The Social Work Pocket

By Rob Harrison and Si

First Edition 2011 ISBN: 978-

A catalogue record for this book will be available from the British Library

©Kirwin Maclean Associates Ltd 4 Mesnes Green, Lichfield, Staffs, WS14 9AB

Printed in Great Britain by Avanti Print Solutions

3

Contents List...

What?

Why?

How?

WHAT?

The concepts of power and empowerment are regularly referred to in social work practice. However, a number of writers have recognised that these concepts are "abstract and ambiguous" and require clarification (for example Deutsch, Coleman and Marcus 2006). This section therefore explores the following questions:

- What is power?
- What is powerlessness?
- What is empowerment?
- How is power constructed?

Considering these questions should help you to understand how power is constructed and carefully consider what is perhaps the most important question of all:

WHAT IS POWER ALL ABOUT?

Defining Power

Defining power is a complex task. As Bernhagen (2002: 1) states it is *"widely unclear whether power should be conceived as an attribute or a relation, as a capacity or a commodity."* It is probably therefore worth beginning the task at a simplistic level by considering dictionary definitions of power, which indicate that power is:

An energy or force

A legal authority to act (where aspects of choice may be removed from other people e.g.: when a crime has been committed, the state has the power to imprison someone)

The possession of qualities (especially mental qualities) which are required to do something or get something done

Political, financial or social force or influence

The capacity of a system or machine to operate

What?

Power is the production of causal effects. It is the bringing about of consequences. (Lukes 1986: 6)

Power is the capacity to affect the behaviour of another – to persuade another to do something that he (sic) would not do on his own. Power is both purpose-driven and leadership-driven in whatever social setting it is applied. (Tuitt 2010)

Power is intrinsic to all social interaction. (Thompson 2001: 89)

Power may comprise anything that establishes and maintains the control of man over man (sic). It applies in all social relationships. (Morgenthau 1978: 8)

9

How is power constructed?

As a complex concept, power is made up of a number of layers or aspects. This can be represented as follows:

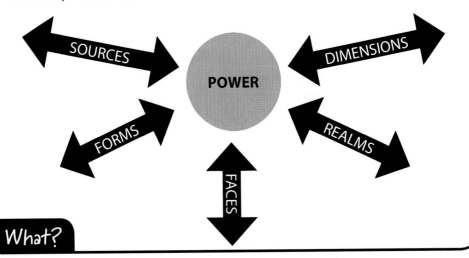

Dimensions of Power: Power over, of and to

Dominelli (2002: 17) refers to French's 1985 definition of three dimensions of power – power over, power of and power to:

Power over refers to the power held by one dominant group over another. This could be around relative social power of certain groups, or it could relate to the power of social workers over service users.

Power of is about the collective strength which people hold to make changes, and this occurs when people come together for such a specific reason or purpose.

Power to is about people's ability to make changes or decisions (also referred to as 'transformative power'). This relates to either individuals or groups.

Dimensions of power: Power with, to and within

Veneklasen and Miller of Just Associates (see for example 2006), have developed the idea of three positive forms of power, which attempts at empowerment need to tap into:

Power with

This is about people finding common ground to build collective strength. Creating power with requires acknowledging diversity and disagreement while seeking common ground around values and actions.

Power to

This recognises the potential of each individual to shape their own life and their own world. It is a concept based on the idea that everyone has the power to make a difference, which can be maximised through individual learning and development. Just Associates argue that recent 'top down' approaches undermine peoples sense of power to.

What?

Power within

This relates to a person's self worth , self knowledge and self esteem. It relies on people having the ability to imagine something differently and to have hope. Spirituality, critical reflection and creative arts can all affirm power within.

Empowerment involves supporting people to develop all three forms of power.

Realms of Power: Public, private and intimate

In considering power as it relates to gender, Veneklasen and Miller (2002) identify the following three realms of power:

Public realm of power
This is visible power seen in employment and public life (where for example men and women are treated differently which is clear from an analysis of gender relations and the widely recognised gender pay gap.)

Private realm of power
This is the power which is expressed within peoples' private lives – for example in family relationships, friendships and intimate relationships.

Intimate realm of power
This is closely linked to the concept of power within – it is about aspects of self esteem, confidence and peoples' relationship to their body.

What?

Forms of Power: Soft Power and Hard Power

This concept is drawn from politics and the writing of Joseph Nye (for example 2004). Despite the fact that its roots lie in the political arena it is a useful concept for understanding forms of power which could be helpful in social work.

HARD POWER

This is about getting people to change their position – it relies on either inducements (carrots) or threats (sticks).

This rests on the ability to shape the preferences of others. According to Nye it is about leading people and modelling what you want them to do. It co-opts people rather than coerces them and is often seen as being based on the ability to get what you want through attraction.

SOFT POWER

15

Faces of Power

Various writers have developed the concept of three different faces of power (VeneKlasen and Miller 2002, Hinson and Healey 2003 and Lukes 2004):

VISIBLE POWER

This is the power that we see – it is essentially about decision making and is reflected in rules, structures and institutions.

HIDDEN POWER

This is the power which is exercised 'behind the scenes' away from the public eye. Essentially it is about agenda setting (relating to the terminology of the 'hidden agenda'). It is reflected in the fact that powerful people, powerful groups and powerful institutions maintain their influence by controlling what gets on the agenda.

What?

INVISIBLE POWER

This is seen as the most insidious of the three faces of power. It is about the way that powerful groups can influence the way that people think (shaping beliefs, peoples' sense of self etc) through processes of socialisation and internalisation. This is well explained by Hinson and Healey (2003:5):

"When those who have the power to name and to socially construct reality choose not to see you or hear you…. when someone with the authority, of a teacher, say, describes the world and you are not in it, there is a moment of psychic disequilibrium, as if you looked in the mirror and saw nothing. It takes some strength of soul – and not just individual strength but collective understanding – to resist this void, this non-being, into which you are thrust, and to stand up, demanding to be seen and heard."

The Power Cube

John Gaventa's model of the Power cube was developed in 1980 as a means of analysing the way in which power works when people try to make changes (Gaventa 2005). Although the origins of this model relate to power within communities, it is also relevant to understanding power in individual contexts.

The Power Cube takes the three faces of power we have described, and interlinks the faces of power (called forms in Gaventa's model) with the levels and spaces within which power operates:

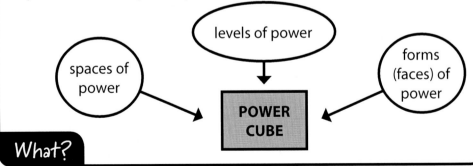

What?

19

The spaces of power are:

Closed spaces: These are the places where decisions are made which are closed off to people who are not in certain groups. Closed spaces could be political, managerial or linked to certain groups, but closed spaces also operate within workplace cultures and social groups.

Invited spaces: People may be invited to participate in decision making in certain spaces. For example, this could be seen in social work in many service user involvement opportunities. The invitations to take part in these spaces though are still controlled to some extent by those with the power to invite or exclude.

Claimed spaces: These are where people claim the right to have their say, to be heard and to make a difference. The development of peer advocacy in social care is a good example of this, as spaces are claimed where people demand that opportunities and closed spaces should be opened up to them so that they can participate in decision making.

What?

Whoever creates the space determines the nature of the decision making that happens in that space.

The levels of power are:

Local: The increase in community based provision, local forums for decision making and local authority determined priorities for service delivery show that the local level is important within the context of social work.

National: Gaventa suggests that the national governmental level is still the most significant level at which change takes place. In social work, this is seen in the extent to which national legislation, governmental priorities and economic pressures create the context within which we work, and within which service user interventions are delivered.

Global: At the global level, there are several bodies who determine the financial, moral and social changes and contexts within which we all live and operate.

How does the Power Cube work?

The idea is that we all operate within these forms, levels and spaces. Our ability to make changes in our own lives is determined by these, and takes place in these contexts. This is the same for the users of social work services, and for the very way in which services are constructed and delivered.

The Power Cube model suggests that power is shifting rather than set, and that the forms, spaces and levels all interact with each other, rather than being static. Changes have to be meaningful at each level, spaces have to be both created and claimed by those who change will affect, and we all need to understand in some way how power exists and operates in various forms to be able to make change possible.

To challenge power, and also to empower service users to do so, "entry points" to the Power Cube need to be found, and several inter-linked approaches need to be taken.

What?

Sources of Power

In a 1959 study which is now seen as a classic, French and Raven identified five sources or types of power:

Legitimate or positional power: This is power that exists because of the way an organisation is structured or through how society is ordered. People have power because of their position within an organisation – for example, a social worker can decide if a person is eligible for a service, and a police officer has the power to arrest someone.

Expert or professional power: This is where a person is seen as having a bank of knowledge or expertise. Social workers have expert power based on their professional training, qualification and experience.

Reward power: This is power gained through the ability to give 'rewards' of some kind. In social work, those who assess and make plans can hold a significant amount of reward power, for example in making decisions about what services can be offered to people.

Referent power: This is power created by the admiration and respect a person can have for another person. This can be based on individual characteristics (or charisma) or it can be based on admiration that people have for people from a particular profession. A good example of this is a person's respect for their GP (although the GP's power is also derived from legitimate and expert power).

Coercive power: This is power based on the ability to apply punishment or sanctions. This power is most keenly felt in children's services (going to court for a care order) and mental health services (around the use of the Mental Health Act). The service user could be conscious of this power even if it has not been actively applied by social workers. Coercive power can be seen as the most obvious form of power and it is perhaps the form of power which is most likely to build resentment or defensiveness from people on the receiving end of it.

What?

The Inner London Probation Service (1993) recognised French and Raven's sources of power, but added two additional sources of power:

Societal power: This is the power based on the ideology of superiority. Some people experience oppression at the hands of others. Oppressors are powerful and oppressed people are less powerful. For example, an older person who experiences ageism will feel less powerful than a younger person.

The power to determine: The Inner London Probation Service examines the power dynamics in practice education and refer to this power as the power a practice educator has to 'pass or fail' a student. In many ways the power to determine, is simply the power to make decisions which determine outcomes for another person. Social workers can have the power to determine in a number of ways – for example in making decisions about action to be taken.

Representations, Modes and Sites of Power

Smith (2010) suggests a layered definition of power within social work as follows:

1. **Representations of Power**

   a. Power as something which is <u>potential</u> as opposed to real.

   b. Power as something which is <u>possessed</u> (e.g.: by dominant groups in society).

   c. Power which is <u>fluid</u> i.e.: something which flows between groups and within individual relationships.

   d. Power which is the <u>product</u> of a relationship between people i.e.: something which **only** comes from people coming together.

Smith suggests that these representations require us to see power as 'multi-dimensional' as opposed to it being a 'thing' which exists in one single form.

What?

2. Modes of Power

a. <u>Personal Power</u> – individual charisma, characteristics and identities.

b. <u>Positional Power</u> – This is similar to French and Raven's (1959) concept of legitimate power, with Smith referring to the concept of authority within certain social roles as key to establishing status and power within social structures.

c. <u>Relational Power</u> – Smith suggests that professionals gain relational power by being effective in their practice in terms of developing trust, credibility and a sense of legitimacy to act on the person's behalf which is granted by the person to the worker.

3. **Sites of Power**

   a. <u>Formal sites</u> (e.g.: court rooms, child protection conferences) are where power is most obviously held and exercised in social work.

   b. <u>Family and home settings</u> – power dynamics within families are determined within the settings and places where families live and interact. Individuals operate according to norms, and some have dominance over others within certain settings.

   c. <u>Community sites</u> – Smith argues that social work could take more opportunities to engage with the potential for community ownership of solutions as communities are the places where people find solidarity, collective identity and local resources.

What?

Powerlessness is:

- A sensation of being out of control with no apparent solution to help regain control
- Complete lack of control, authority or status to affect how others will treat or act towards you
- Lack of strength, competence or skills to overcome realities in life that have no current apparent solution.
(Live Strong 2011)

Although obvious, powerlessness is best defined as the absence of power and control in your own life. People often feel a lack of power, influence, strength or ability around choices in their own life, the difficulties they face and the means to resolve these.
(Maclean and Harrison 2010)

29

Factors which restrict people's sense of their own power

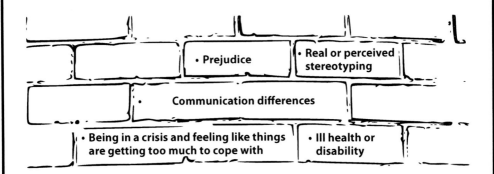

- Prejudice
- Real or perceived stereotyping
- Communication differences
- Being in a crisis and feeling like things are getting too much to cope with
- Ill health or disability

What?

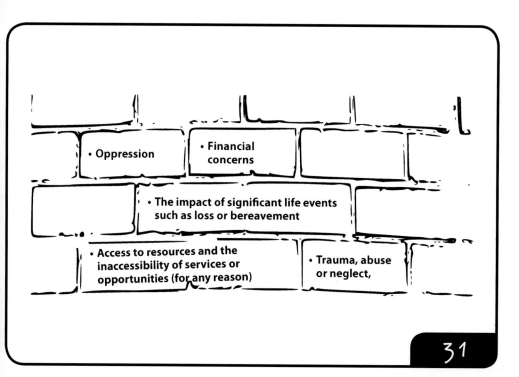

- Oppression
- Financial concerns
- The impact of significant life events such as loss or bereavement
- Access to resources and the inaccessibility of services or opportunities (for any reason)
- Trauma, abuse or neglect,

31

Empowerment is:

Intimately connected with individuals feelings of self worth and self confidence and sense of efficacy..... it is also inseparably linked to the social and political conditions in which people live.
(Kreisberg 1992: 19)

The process by which individuals and groups gain power, access to resources and control over their own lives. In doing so, they gain the ability to achieve the highest personal and collective aspirations and goals.
(Robbins, Chatterjee and Canda 1998: 91)

The process of helping individuals, families, groups and communities to increase their personal, interpersonal, socio-economic and political strength to develop influence toward improving their circumstances.
(Barker 2009)

What?

Freire

The Brazilian educator Paulo Freire is well known for his writing on empowerment. His book 'The Pedagogy of the Oppressed' (first published in English in 1970) is seen as a seminal text. Freire saw empowerment as being created rather than being 'given'. He viewed empowerment as being about:

Power in learning being shared between individuals

A means and an outcome in itself

Leading to a 'collective critical consciousness' (ie: groups of people critIcise an institutionalised perspective on what education involves, and work together to adapt and improve this)

Liberatory for individuals

Focused on social change through collective action

33

The imagery and language about power is around construction. This is perhaps very fitting as feeling disempowered can be like feeling there is an insurmountable brick wall ahead of you.

Social work literature often refers to the social work 'toolbox' of skills. Empowerment begins by understanding how the brick wall of exclusion is constructed – so that the social worker can make use of their skills to 'deconstruct' the brick wall.

What?

WHY?

Smith (2010) asserts that a *"clear understanding of and strategy for dealing with power and its consequences are important components of the practitioner's toolkit."*

In exploring the following questions:

- Why are power and empowerment important concepts in social work?

- What are the benefits of empowerment?

- Why do social workers find empowerment challenging?

This section should help you to identify why power and empowerment are such key issues in social work practice.

WHY IS EMPOWERMENT SO IMPORTANT IN SOCIAL WORK PRACTICE?

Why do social workers need to develop their understanding of power and empowerment?

Power is always an issue for social workers

Empowerment requires a clear understanding of power dynamics and how disempowered service users can be

Social workers may well misunderstand power and empowerment

Effective support for service users relies on practitioners having a well developed understanding of power and empowerment

Why?

Contemporary policy and likely future changes to social work are based on issues of power and empowerment

Safeguarding is a central role for social workers – power and its misuse are key issues in safeguarding practice

Empowerment lies at the heart of social work practice

Social work practice can be disempowering, especially where practitioners lack awareness of power and empowerment

Social workers work with people who are disempowered

Power and social work

Foucault (1977: 27) identified that power is everywhere and comes from everywhere. Certainly the major impact that power has on society has long been recognised. For example in 1942 Spykman said *"Without mechanical power – the ability to move mass – there can be no technology. Without political power – the ability to move men (sic) – technology cannot serve a social purpose. All civilized life rests, therefore, in the last instance on power"*. (Spykman 1942: 11)

Clearly, since power is so pervasive in society, social workers need to develop a clear understanding of power and the potential impact of this on the lives of service users and on their practice. As Cooper (2011: 20) states:

"Social work is essentially about power...... interventions into others' lives is an intervention into networks of power relationships. It is the structures of power and powerlessness that produce both the problems and the potential solutions."

Why?

Practitioners do not always recognise the power issues in their work. Sometimes practitioners only reflect on power issues when they are explicit, and 'in your face', missing the importance of power in <u>every</u> situation.

Issues of power are real and embedded in practice and cannot be sidelined or treated as subordinate questions to be dealt with only if time permits.

(Smith 2010)

Power is intrinsic to all social interaction - we cannot escape the significance of it in our dealings with people.

(Thompson 2001)

Having an understanding of the impact of power in practice could not be described in itself as empowerment, but it might be described as 'power sensitive' practice (Gardner 2011) and it is the first vital step towards empowerment.

Contemporary practice and policy development

Contemporary social work practice has rejected the idea of the professional gift model of support and is working towards the concept of empowerment (Social Platform 2010: 1).

In the early part of this century, the labour Government developed what it referred to as the empowerment agenda. This led on to what is often described as a 'frenetic period' of policy development in social work and related sectors.

At the time of writing the Coalition Government is promoting the idea of the Big Society which they describe as based on community empowerment – in terms of the transfer of power from central government to local communities (Chanan and Miller 2010).

Why?

Concepts of self directed care, self assessment, co-production and personalisation are all part of contemporary practice and appear in the policy directions setting out visions for the future of social work.

Change which is imposed and isn't well explained can lead to people feeling disempowered, and the pace of change in contemporary social work can certainly lead to confusion. Anticipating change can be helpful to social workers in managing the seemingly constant changes to practice. You may feel like you need a crystal ball to anticipate change! At the very least, it is helpful to have a well developed understanding of power and empowerment to anticipate likely changes to social work policy and the impact of these on practice.

The Scottish Government (2005) identify that understanding power and its fluid nature is vital in understanding the likely changes to social work practice in the 21st Century.

Social Work is built on empowerment

The International definition of social work demonstrates the centrality of empowerment in social work practice:

"The social work profession promotes social change, problem solving in human relationships and the empowerment and liberation of people to enhance well-being. Utilising theories of human behaviour and social systems, social work intervenes at the points where people interact with their environments. Principles of human rights and social justice are fundamental to social work."

(IFSW and IASSW 2000)

This international definition of social work is currently under review and perhaps the most heated aspect of the debate has revolved around social work and empowerment. Many statutory social workers have talked about the way that their abilities to work in a truly empowering way has been increasingly limited over the years by proceduralised managerial practice.

Why?

The review of the definition has certainly highlighted a Global diversity in understandings about contemporary empowerment practice.

Understanding power dynamics and the impact that these have on peoples' lives arguably remains one thing that sets social work apart from other professions. Higham (2005) states that one of the things which makes social work a unique profession is that it builds on an *"awareness of structural oppression, power, service users' rights and responsibilities and social inclusion."*

It is clear, therefore that power and empowerment are key issues in social work practice. Since we refer regularly to the 'construction' of power, it is fitting to talk about social work being built on power.

Social workers work with people who are disempowered

Hepworth et al (2010: 14) highlight the fact that social workers work with *"...individuals, groups and entire communities who lack the power of self determination..."* They go on to explain that *"indeed the powerless are more likely to have government agencies and public policy exert significant authority in their lives."*

This can lead to a vicious cycle where the more disempowered people are, the more others exert their power.

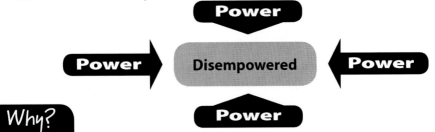

Why?

Fook (2002: 51) suggests that people can often be disempowered by the 'best intentions' of professionals. Sometimes, doing too much for someone can lead to the 'learned helplessness' effect occurring, to dependencies being created, and to workers' own needs to be the 'helper' being catered for, as opposed to the service users' need to be in control of their own life.

Kam (2002) highlighted the fact that social workers often unintentionally disempower older people through negative attitudes towards ageing, the use of the medical model, denying older people the right to participate in decision making and limiting options for choice and control.

If social workers do not have a well developed understanding of power, powerlessness and empowerment not only are they unlikely to be able to support service users effectively, but they may also further disempower service users who are already powerless.

45

Safeguarding and Empowerment

Safeguarding is a central component of social work practice in every field of practice (see for example, GSCC 2009 and SCIE 2009). In order to safeguard people, social workers must have a clear understanding of power.

Power and abuse are linked in many ways.

- Abuse involves a misuse of power. For example, the NSPCC (2011) highlight the fact that *"child abuse....... is an abuse of power."*
- Many victims of abuse are in some kind of relationship with their abuser which involves a power dynamic.
- Social workers can feel powerless in their work to prevent abuse.

The Duluth model of domestic violence (online 2011) which has been developed since the early 1980s highlights the way that power and control are central to domestic violence.

Why?

(For further details see www.theduluthmodel.org)

47

It is now widely recognised that since power and abuse are so inextricably linked, empowerment can be a very effective method of safeguarding. For example:

- White et al (2003) identified empowerment as a key component to safeguarding adults in residential care from abuse and exploitation.
- The Department of Health (2009) found that in terms of adult safeguarding, empowerment is a protective factor against abuse and identified evidence that shifting the power balance within families and between service users and professionals can have very positive safeguarding outcomes.
- Kendrick (1998) explored some of the issues around the abuse of children in care and recognised empowerment practice as key to safeguarding, especially in terms of prevention.
- Warrin (2010) claims that the effective integration of safeguarding and empowerment contains the '"seeds for a transformation of care" with regard to the prevention of abuse and neglect.
- The CSCI (2008) see empowering individuals as a crucial factor in safeguarding.

Why?

Kendrick (1998) identified the following key steps in protecting children in care:

- ✓ Listen to the person
- ✓ Provide access to helplines
- ✓ Provide opportunities for peer support, and peer advocacy
- ✓ Provide access to independent advocates
- ✓ Involve the service user in all planning and decision making about their life
- ✓ Involve service users in staff recruitment and selection
- ✓ Ensure better staff training and embed whistle blowing policies
- ✓ Involve family members and the wider community (eg: Independent Visitors) where possible

Notice how similar these are to the key elements of empowerment?

What are the benefits of empowerment?

Croft and Beresford (1992) assert that empowerment creates mutual respect between practitioners and the users of services. Certainly, empowerment has major benefits for both service users and practitioners:

<u>Benefits to service users</u>

- ✓ Raises self esteem
- ✓ Enables people to mobilise their own resources
- ✓ Reduces isolation
- ✓ Reduces risk and the likelihood of abuse occurring
- ✓ Makes the person feel that professionals are working with them as opposed to "doing to" them
- ✓ Reduces the potential creation of dependency on services and professionals, and "learned helplessness"

Why?

<u>Benefits to practitioners</u>

- ✓ Provides a very practical focus or "recipe" for practice
- ✓ Leads to increased job satisfaction
- ✓ Enables better assessment and planning to take place
- ✓ Ensures the outcomes of work with people can be monitored and shared more accurately
- ✓ Can enable new services to be developed around people's own view of their needs
- ✓ Can reduce potential risk to people and isolation of individuals
- ✓ Enables workers to learn from each other's practices and develop an evidence base for good practice

There are many benefits to empowerment for both practitioners and service users

51

Why do social workers find empowerment challenging?

Despite the fact that empowerment is an essential component of social work practice, practitioners can be challenged by it. The reasons for this include:

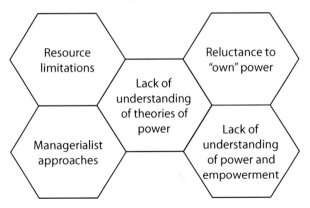

Resource limitations

Lack of understanding of theories of power

Reluctance to "own" power

Managerialist approaches

Lack of understanding of power and empowerment

Why?

Managerialist approaches

Managerialism and empowerment are closely linked, in two main ways:

Managerialism is about a shift in power: Clarke et al (2000) define managerialism as an approach which disregards professionalism and undermines localised democracy by placing the power firmly in the hands of central government. Whilst Governments argue that current policy focuses on devolving power, the setting of performance targets and progress measurement does place power in the hands of central government.

Managerialism constrains empowerment: Smith (2010) asserts that managerialist practice constrains social workers with an empowerment focus. The procedural focus of contemporary practice certainly makes empowerment much more challenging for practitioners.

Resource limitations and the current financial climate

Resources are always finite, but over recent years resource limitations have had an increasing impact on social work provision (see for example Walker and Beckett 2003, Betts Adams, Matto and Lecroy 2009 and Zastrow 2010).

As Rodgers (2003: 93) asserts *"Power is scarce, unequal and often coercive, which tends to lead to conflict over access to finite resources."* The current financial climate within which we operate will have an impact on power and empowerment in various ways.

The International Federation of Social Workers (2011) have recognised the significant impact of the current global financial crisis on social work. They highlight that it has had a major impact on the availability of resources and services at a time when more people are actually in need of support.

Social workers often follow the traditional model of social work / case management, characterised by assessment followed by the provision of

Why?

services. Where they have limited or no resources to offer service users, social workers can feel that they cannot empower service users and may themselves feel disempowered. However, it is important to recognise that a good quality assessment can be an 'end' in itself, not necessarily leading to intervention.

"While assessment is sometimes viewed as preceding intervention, increasingly assessment is being seen as a service in its own right rather than as a prelude to service delivery." (SCIE 2003: 2)

With the current financial crisis and limited resources, social workers often feel pushed into focussing on peoples needs and stressing difficulties. This will further disempower service users. It is important that social workers do not go into an assessment with a negative defeatist attitude feeling that "I can't offer anything anyway." This simply leads to a service led approach. Instead, social workers should work towards supporting service users to recognise and build on their strengths, acknowledging the service user as the expert on their own situation. By taking such an approach, social workers can empower service users rather than leaving them further disempowered.

Lack of understanding of power and empowerment

Power is incredibly complex which can lead to either misunderstandings or a simplistic view of power which misses a number of key issues. Some of the common misunderstandings around power in social work include:

Power is viewed as the same for everyone

Different people, groups, cultures, and individuals (including within the social work profession) have different understandings of what power is, what equality and inequality means, and therefore what needs to occur to address this. This has the effect that we can sometimes misunderstand the nature of people's issues and disempowerment, which leads to our values and cultural norms being imposed upon those we seek to empower. Recognising and celebrating diversity is therefore a key aspect of empowerment practice as is understanding your own definitions and understanding of power.

Why?

Power is seen as wholly negative

Power is very often negatively viewed by social workers. This may be because social workers so often see and work with the consequences of abuse and significant misuse of power. It might also be based on a misunderstanding of empowerment and social workers wrongly feeling that they should not have power. It is important to remember though that:

"Nothing is innately wrong with the word power, but it has commonly been used in contexts that have given it monstrous connotations. To many people, power conjures visions of autocracy….. many think of power in terms of brute force, cunning, hatred and injustice." (Shivers 2001: 133)

Power can in fact be used to achieve positive change and it is vital that both the negative and positive sides of power are recognised by social workers. Where power is viewed entirely negatively, practitioners will not be comfortable about their power – which is an essential aspect of empowerment.

Power is understood simply as a commodity

As we have seen there is considerable debate about whether power is an attribute, capacity or commodity (e.g. Bernhagen 2002). Fook (2002: 48) suggests that social work has traditionally understood power as a commodity, meaning that:

- It is viewed as something which social workers possess

- Power is viewed as being transferred from one person to another

- If the social worker transfers power to service users, this leaves the worker as the person who is disempowered

- There is a limited quantity of power which means that we have to make choices about who to empower, and base these choices on who we feel is most disadvantaged by their lack of power

It is important that practitioners develop their awareness of power and recognise that it is much more than a simple commodity.

Why?

Denial of Power

Very often when we talk to social workers and social care workers about power and ask them to identify their power, they struggle to do so. In fact they often identify how powerless they feel.

There may be a number of reasons for this:

- Managerialist approaches to social work can leave practitioners feeling powerless
- Social workers may feel uncomfortable with owning power and so internalise a denial of power
- Empowerment may have been misunderstood – such that social workers feel they should not talk about the power they own
- Power is often negatively viewed by practitioners who then feel less able to articulate the power they have

> *The more power that social workers have, the less they seem ready or able to own that power.* (ILPS 1993)

> *Ironically often the people best able to identify power, the way it operates and the impact it has are those who are powerless.* (ILPS 1993)

Understanding why empowerment is important and what the challenges might be are key to practice implementation. This section of the Pocket Guide has highlighted the fact that there are many reasons why empowerment is important to effective social work practice.

Perhaps the most important reason of all is that:

"Where practitioners lack an understanding of power and empowerment service users are left more vulnerable to abuse."

(Association of Directors of Social Services 2005)

The question remains how can social workers operating in the current climate actualise their aims in terms of empowerment?

Why?

HOW?

The Pocket Guide 'What? Why? How?' format is probably more important for this subject than any other since it is impossible to *do* the 'how' (empowering practice) unless you understand the 'what' (how power is constructed) and the 'why' (why are people disempowered). This section explores the main components of empowerment, by considering the following questions:

- Is empowerment aspirational or achievable?
- How can social workers apply the concept of empowerment to their practice?

By considering the key components of empowerment practice this section of the pocket guide should help you to explore:

HOW CAN I PUT EMPOWERMENT INTO PRACTICE?

Empowerment : aspiration or reality?

The barriers to empowerment (including the managerialist agenda in current social work practice) mean that empowerment is challenging for contemporary social workers. As a result, Gardner (2011) asserts that it may be better to see empowerment as an *"aspirational rather than attainable goal."*

Whilst understanding Gardner's view, we believe that there are aspects of empowerment which are attainable in contemporary social work practice.

Many writers describe social work theories as 'recipes' for practice (see for example Lopez 2011). In considering theories and models then, we think it can be useful to take the 'ingredients' into account.

Empowerment can be seen as an abstract concept. Viewing empowerment as a recipe and considering the key ingredients can make it more concrete and therefore assist practitioners in working in an empowering way.

How?

The best cooks adapt recipes taking into account the ingredients they have at hand, such that the dish they produce will turn out differently each time. We feel that empowerment can be used in practice whatever the limitations are, where the concept is broken down into its components (or ingredients). In this way, a social worker committed to empowerment can put the key components into practice, whatever challenges they face - adapting the 'recipe', by taking into account the ingredients and equipment available and the unique nature of each service user's situation.

SPICE

Empowerment: Micro, Meso or Macro?

These terms are often used when referring to empowerment practice, so it is worth having a clear understanding of what they mean. The concept of three different levels is drawn from sociology where practice viewed on a three level basis. The three different levels represent groupings of society based on their scale, as follows:

Micro: The 'smallest' level. Micro level practice can be seen as working with more 'intimate' levels of society: in social work this may relate to work with individuals or families.

Meso: This is the less well known 'middle level' of practice. It can be seen as relating to groups and small neighbourhoods or communities.

Macro: This is the larger grouping such as whole communities or very large groups - for example all women.

macro

meso

micro

How?

Social work itself can be viewed as being practised on micro, meso or macro levels. The current National Occupational Standards, for example, refer to working with individuals, families (micro?), groups (meso?) and communities (macro?)

We come from the understanding that empowerment can take place on a micro, meso or macro level - in that individuals, families, groups or communities can be empowered.

Each of the key components of empowerment covered in this section could be used on any of the three levels, although it is worth recognising that:

- some of the 'methods' are generally used more on one level than another
- some of the methods are easier to use on a meso or macro level than on a micro level

As a practitioner, you need to consider your role and the context of your practice and the agency in which you work when looking at whether you can empower people on a micro, meso or macro level.

65

Empowerment involves:

Understanding the construction of power

Seeing the service user as the expert

Owning power and using it responsibly

Encouraging hopefulness

Facilitating user involvement

Recognising power differentials

Developing positive attitudes and practice

Acknowledging the dignity of risk and managing risk proactively

Viewing problems as the way in which we develop resilience, as opposed to insurmountable difficulties

How?

Connecting with others who have faced similar issues to then be able to achieve broader collective and social change

Helping service users to develop resources

Exchanging information

Drawing on the strengths perspective

Addressing inequality

Enabling and facilitating learning

Listening and hearing

Rejecting the idea that problems develop because of personal inadequacy

Assuming personal responsibility

67

Understanding the construction of power

As can be seen from the What? section of this Pocket Guide, power is a complex and dynamic concept. The first and perhaps most important step in empowerment is to understand the way that power is constructed and to be clear about what power means to you as an individual. A poorly developed understanding of power can certainly lead to an abuse of that power.

Understanding power as the starting point for empowerment is widely recognised. For example, Bar-On (2002) asserts that social workers must increase their understanding of power and its dynamics if they are to effectively support those people that society excludes and makes vulnerable.

One of the issues in understanding power is that much of the way in which power is written about is based on a dichotomy of 'either / or'. Fook (2002: 49) calls this 'binary oppositional relations'.

For example, social workers with an underdeveloped understanding about the complexities of power may believe:

How?

- People are either powerful **or** powerless:
  - Social workers hold the power, and therefore service users have none
  - Some in society hold power because of their ethnicity, gender, sexuality etc, and others have less
  - Managers hold the power in many social work settings around resources, and social workers often feel powerless to do the work which brought them into the profession in the first place
- Power held by social workers is either good **or** bad:
  - Good: For society in keeping people safe; for the service user in having a system to turn to in times of stress or crisis; for the social worker in having a basis for decision making etc
  - Bad: For service users if their choices are restricted, or if certain actions need to take place in order to keep a person safe; for social workers in having to take actions which others perceive as negative etc
  - People need either Care **or** Control
  - Expertise lies with either the practitioner **or** the service user

69

The concept of empowerment is based on the need for these concepts to be harmonised, as opposed to set up as incompatible opposites to each other in these ways. It is therefore vital that social work practitioners recognise where they stand in terms of their understanding of power – how do they see power and how can they harmonise with opposing views so that they can work in an empowering way?

It is important to recognise that:

- People can be **both** powerful **and** powerless (in different situations, for example).
- Power can be **both** positive **and** negative - it is the way that power is used which makes it 'good or bad'.
- In some situations we may need a balance of **both** care **and** control.
- Service users are the experts on their own life and their situation. However, professionals may have expertise on the process of finding solutions or on how to navigate services which service users may not have.

How?

You need to find a way to harmonise opposing views.

Owning Power

Social workers can be uncomfortable with power, such that they do not see themselves as powerful. However, in order to empower others, it is important to have power - and a vital part of this is recognising and owning power. Alice Walker (undated online) states that *"the most common way people give up their power is by thinking they don't have any."*

The following poem demonstrates the need for each of us, as individuals, to own our power:

> It is our light not our darkness that most frightens us
> Our deepest fear is not that we are inadequate.
> Our deepest fear is that we are powerful beyond measure.
> It is our light not our darkness that most frightens us.
> We ask ourselves, who am I to be brilliant, gorgeous,
> talented and fabulous?

How?

Actually, who are you not to be?
You are a child of God.
Your playing small does not serve the world.
There's nothing enlightened about shrinking so that other
people won't feel insecure around you.

We were born to make manifest the glory of
God that is within us.
It's not just in some of us; it's in everyone.
And as we let our own light shine,
we unconsciously give other people
permission to do the same.

As we are liberated from our own fear,
Our presence automatically liberates others.

Marianne Williamson (1992)

Using Power Responsibly

In order to make responsible use of the power that they have, it is vital that social workers:

- Understand the nature of their power

- Reflect on their communication, and the way in which they present themselves and the power they hold to the people they work with

- Seek to understand each person as a unique individual, recognising the factors which oppress them or which restrict their access to resources and opportunities

- Reflect on the choices they offer to service users, and the factors influencing their assessment and planning

- Explain their actions in a way which shows that their decision making has been considerate, respectful, informed by knowledge and evidence, and therefore legitimate (sometimes referred to as defensible decision making).

> *The problem with power is not power itself, it is how to achieve its responsible use.*
> (Robert F. Kennedy. Online undated)

How?

Be aware of how you exercise power

The use of power is also about how it is exercised. Two examples of how people can exercise their power lie in the way they dress and the language they use.

Power dressing

There is considerable debate in social work about what social workers should wear and we know students who say that their most lively group discussions during their courses have been on this topic. Snell (2007) argues that social workers should dress 'down':

"What could be more alienating for a service user who doesn't have a bean to their name to be confronted with a professional dressed up to the nines who makes them feel even more down on their luck than they were feeling already. Power dressing should be banished to the boardroom where it belongs."

We don't personally have any strong feelings about how social workers should dress, the problem we have with this debate is really about the language that is used around it – the whole concept of dressing 'up' and 'down' means that there are class or power connotations to whichever decision an individual worker reaches about whether to dress "up or down". Certainly the way you dress does have an impact on power dynamics and it is something that practitioners should reflect on when they are considering their approach to empowerment.

Language and power
Mooney et al (2011) make clear that language can be used to exercise power. Language creates barriers between people, it can disempower, dehumanise and ultimately depersonalise.

<u>Depersonalisation</u>: 'ic' is often added to a diagnosis to describe someone – diabetic, schizophrenic etc. This is incredibly depersonalising. It is much more personalised and ultimately empowering to refer to someone as living with a diagnosis of diabetes rather than as 'a diabetic'.

How?

<u>Dehumanisation:</u> The process of dehumanisation is about people not being seen as a valued human being or the worth of a person being reduced so that they are seen as not quite human (sub-human). Language in social care and social work is very often de-humanising. Perhaps the best example of this is the language used around personal care. For example, people generally 'eat' but as soon as someone comes into contact with social care services they will be referred to as 'feeding themselves' or needing to be 'fed'. In other situations we only refer to feeding about babies and animals. The central message received by people is that they are now less than human.

Many social workers using traditional assessment forms use this language without a second thought. If you are honest, as a social worker how many times have you asked someone if they can feed themselves? Changing the language that we use as practitioners is a very practical first step in respecting people as unique individuals and seeking to empower people.

Seeing service users as experts

Seeing the service user as the expert on their own situation is a key aspect of a range of contemporary social work theories. The strengths perspective includes this as a key component and an understanding of this perspective can be very helpful in empowering people.

The strengths perspective came about partly as a reaction against two features of traditional social work and the provision of health and social care.

1. An increasing medical classification and diagnosis of individuals which leads to labelling of large sections of society.

2. Assessments are weighted towards listing people's deficits, vulnerabilities and negative past experiences. In the current environment where demand for services is increasing but the resources available have been cut, there is an increased focus and heightening of service users' lack of capability and risks.

How?

In both of these suggestions, there is a structural or bureaucratic bias against recognising people's strengths, abilities and resilience. Professionals may be led to make use of a language that is pathologising and alienating in order to ensure that service users have access to services.

Saleebey (1996) generated the following comparison of professional pathologising against the strengths perspective:

Pathology	Strengths
Person is defined as a 'case'. Symptoms add up to a diagnosis.	Person is defined as unique. Traits, talents, resources add up to strengths
Intervention is problem focussed.	Intervention is possibility focussed.
Service user accounts are filtered by a professional to aid the generation of a diagnosis.	Personal accounts are the essential route to knowing and appreciating the person.
Professional is sceptical of personal stories and explanations.	Professional knows the person from the inside out.

Pathology	Strengths
Childhood trauma is the pre cursor or predictor of adult dysfunction.	Childhood trauma is not predictive; it may weaken or strengthen the individual.
Professional devises treatment or care plan.	Focus is aspirations of individual, family or community.
Professional is the expert on service user's life.	Individual, family or community are the experts.
Possibilities for choice, control, commitment and personal development are limited by label / diagnosis or condition.	Possibilities for choice, control, commitment and personal development are open.
Professionals' knowledge, skills and connections are principal resources for service user.	The strength, capacities and adaptive skills of the individual, family or community are the principle resources.

How?

Pathology	Strengths
Support is centred on reducing the effects of symptoms and the negative effects of emotions or relationships.	Support is focussed on getting on with one's life, affirming and developing values and commitments and making or finding membership in a community.

Rankin (2006) identifies the following as key aspects of the strengths perspective in social work:

- **Every person, family and community** *has* **strengths** (it sounds obvious, but how often do people get 'bogged down' in seeing individuals as 'difficult'?) Professionals need to suspend their disbelief about people, just as much as service users and family members may need to do so about their own abilities. The professional role is seen as one which enables people to achieve this by focusing on their strengths and resources.

- **Trauma, abuse and difficulties can be hurtful, but may also be sources of challenge and opportunity** ("if it doesn't kill you, it makes you stronger").

Resilience, independence, loyalty to one or more people can arise due to a painful or traumatic personal experience. People can develop great insight into their own situation.

- **There are no "upper limits" to people's abilities to grow and change,** so we should take people's individual and collective goals seriously.

- **We are most helpful to people when we work *with* them.** Most professionals will probably say that they already apply the strengths perspective to their work. However, the strengths perspective calls on the professional to move away from the objective, concrete and tangible. Professionals have to connect with the individuals they work with in a manner that recognises hope, aspirations, spirituality, identity and belonging. This connection needs to be rooted in a true sense of equality.

- **Every situation and context is full of resources and opportunities.** The social worker is required to enable the service user to recognise the talents, resources, adaptive skills and support network which they have.

How?

- **The concept of community is key to understanding and developing strengths.** The literature highlights dialogue, collaboration and membership of networks as key to successful strengths based approaches.

- **People's own ideas, priorities and solutions are what we should work from.** If we don't do this, then we won't meet that person's needs effectively. even if someone's own solution may not be what we as 'experts' think is best, it is better for the person to develop a solution for themselves as they know themselves better than we ever will. Also, people are more likely to stick to a plan they feel belongs to them than one which feels imposed upon them by others. Solution focused brief therapy and Family Group Conferencing are two practical examples of methodologies which put this into practice.

Resilience

Resilience refers to supporting people develop their own reservoir of skills, abilities and knowledge. Resilience is not about ignoring the real challenges people face, but it does involve acknowledging people's own resources, abilities and ways of getting through these challenges.

Rankin (2006) states:

"Resilience is a process - the continuing growth and articulation of capacities, knowledge, insight, and virtues derived through meeting the demands and challenges of one's world, however chastening."

The resilience perspective recognises that individuals can have difficulties in one area of their life. One of the ways a person overcomes a difficulty is by drawing on other aspects of their life, either directly to problem solve or indirectly so that the person has a sense that in other areas of their life they are doing well.

How?

What develops resilience?

Resilience is sometimes seen as a personal characteristic. However, there are steps which can help people to develop their 'resolve':

- Contact with other people in a similar situation
- Access to others who care about us in a genuine way
- Developing a strong personal support network
- Feeling that we have solved an issue before - this makes us more likely to feel able to cope next time we face something similar
- Praise and recognition of our achievements
- Acknowledgement of our strengths, uniqueness, talents and qualities
- Trying something new or feeling we are learning new skills
- A strong sense of identity, including our cultural and personal resources
- People seeing us as the expert about ourselves

Notice how similar these steps are to the key components of empowerment?

Listening and Hearing

Empowerment relies on the development of empathic holistic relationships. Tolan (2003) describes this type of relationship as one where the practitioner is able to "see the whole world as the other person sees it and is wholly accepting of that world". The foundation of such relationships is active listening – not only through traditional listening to 'words' but also through the use of observational skills. The following poem written by a person with learning disabilities illustrates the importance of active listening:

> To work with me,
> You have to listen to me
> And you can't just listen with your ears.
> Because it will go to your head to fast.
> You have to listen with your whole body.
> If you listen slow, some of what I say
> Will enter your heart

(written by a Canadian student with learning disabilities – source unknown)

How?

The vital importance of active listening to empowerment is recognised by the Yorkshire and Humber Empowerment Partnership (2011: 28) who state that *"we need to practice genuine listening, and not hearing what we think we want to hear."*

In fact, effective listening is very powerful in itself, as Buscaglia (online undated) states: *"too often we underestimate the power of a listening ear".*

Working on the basis that social work is built on empowerment, remember that many of the foundations of empowerment are the basic skills of social work.

SKILL BOX

Information and Empowerment

The concept of providing information as a method of empowerment is probably built on the well known term first coined by Francis Bacon, a 17th century philosopher:

Knowledge is power

Penhale and Parker (2008) recognise the vital importance of providing information to service users. With the rise in the use of information technology Matthews et al (2011) recognise that a key part of the provision of information for service users is ensuring that people have access to information technology.

A key part of an empowerment focussed practitioner's role is recognising the importance of information in empowerment. Aspects of this are more complex than simply the *provision* of information. For example, Seabury, Seabury and Garvin (2011: 130) state that:

How?

"The only power base that a client brings into the relationship is informational. The client has control over much of the information that makes up his or her situation, yet this base may be weakened when a worker enters the situation after consulting with significant others who already know the client."

The relationship between information and empowerment then should be seen as a two way one. When thinking about providing information, consider:

- What information does the person want and need?
- Is this available in a accessible manner?
- What might be the best way to provide this information?
- Does the person have access to ICT?

When thinking about obtaining information, consider:

- What information do I need?
- Why?
- What would be the most empowering way to obtain this information?

The relationship between information and empowerment is a two way one.

Enabling and facilitating learning

Education has long been viewed as a key element of empowerment, and this was reinforced by Friere's writing in the 1970s. In the UK, this aspect of empowerment practice has largely focussed on community education and developing community participation (Yorkshire and Humber Empowerment Partnership 2011) although in many European countries social pedagogy focuses on empowering individuals through lifelong learning.

Social pedagogy has a long history in many European countries – particularly Denmark, France, Italy, Germany and the Netherlands. The UK Government is now recognising the role of social pedagogues and showing an increasing interest in this approach in Government policy (particularly in relation to Children's services). The historical roots of social pedagogy are about taking an individualised educational approach with people to support their learning. Essentially the approach is about educating people in a way which recognises their role as active learners, so that they can take a full and active role in an inclusive society.

How?

Empowerment is a key concept and aim in social pedagogy. Methods for achieving this include:

- Promoting each individuals' well being
- Holistic learning
- Focussing on individuals even in group settings
- Positive empowering and professional relationships between the professional and the person accessing services

Whilst there are very few social pedagogues in the UK at present, it is a growing field of interest and certainly aspects of the pedagogy role can be drawn on by social workers seeking to empower service users.

Cameron (2007) states that *"The social pedagogue works with the whole person, and supports their all-round development. Pedagogues employ theories, professional knowledge, and creative and practical skills with groups and on an individual basis. They acknowledge uncertainty and constantly review situations and decisions, in dialogue with colleagues. Human rights and participation underpin social pedagogy."*

One key aspect of social pedagogy is encouraging service users to reflect on their life situation and experiences and to see these as opportunities for learning *"the power of experiencing something positive – something that makes us happy, something we have achieved, a new skills we have learned, the caring support from someone else.....raises our self-confidence and feeling of self worth, so it reinforces our sense of well being, of learning, of being able to form strong relationships, or of feeling empowered."* (ThemPra 2009)

Napier (undated online) refers to a social worker taking on a teacher / trainer role in empowerment. She argues that this 'primary' role involves two main aspects with:

- a social worker managing the learning process aimed at helping service users find solutions for their situations.
- a social worker acting as a broker to seek to educate professionals and communities about the barriers that people encounter.

How?

Personal Commitment

The vital importance of practitioners having a personal commitment to empowerment practice is widely acknowledged (see for example Beirne 2006).

Lum (2010) recognises that whilst empowerment requires *"social transformation on a massive scale"*, it must begin with each individual having a personal commitment to empowerment and to making a difference.

To work in an empowering way it is therefore vital that you reflect on your personal commitment to empowerment. How committed are you? How do you demonstrate this in your practice?

Friere (1970) stated that *"washing ones hands of the conflict between the powerful and the powerless means to side with the powerful, not to be neutral."*

Facilitating User Involvement

Involving service users in every aspect of service provision is a vital aspect of empowerment in social work. Service users must be meaningfully involved in all aspects of the service, such as:

- assessment and care processes (through self assessment or co-production)
- service provision
- service development
- future service planning
- wider discussions about care services

Gallagher (2010: 2) states that user involvement can be seen on two levels:

"First there is the engagement of the social worker with the client in the business of carrying out social work. Second there is the more consultative or participative understanding of engagement as the process of eliciting the views of users about what they want from social services, with the aim of listening to and responding to these views."

How?

On a group level, many services and service providers are beginning to recognise the need to encourage service user participation and have responded to this in various ways through actions such as:

- involving service users in management groups and service planning groups
- involving service users in interviews, induction and training and education
- setting up service user consultation groups
- user groups managing particular aspects of service delivery
- peer reviews
- co-production of assessments and care plans
- surveys and focus groups
- User development of charters and standards for delivery

People think the only thing we know is how to moan. But they are not listening. We know what needs changing, what works and what doesn't work. We know this because we live it 24/7, 52 weeks a year with no days off.
(Service user in Branfield and Beresford 2006)

Research (eg: Branfield and Beresford 2006) indicates that two activities are central to making user involvement work:

1. People being able to get together to work collectively for change and mutual support
2. Service users knowledge, experience, views and ideas being listened to and valued.

This leaves us with the chicken and egg question - user involvement is empowering, but how do we empower people so that they can effectively engage in consultation? Which comes first? Again this demonstrates the complexity of empowerment.

How?

Comments and Complaints Procedures

Comments and complaints procedures are an essential aspect of giving service users a voice and working towards empowerment.

An effective complaints procedure is essential for service users, but it can also be helpful for practitioners in that an effective complaints procedure can:

- bring attention to lack of resources
- emphasise the need for a high quality service provision
- identify areas of poor practice
- support staff to develop their practice
- clarify misunderstandings
- ensure that service user's concerns are appropriately directed rather than creating conflict within the professional relationship
- challenge the status-quo
- test and improve systems and processes

It is therefore important that social care professionals do not view complaints procedures negatively or as a threat. A good quality complaints procedure is a positive attribute to a service. It will encourage recipients of the service to participate more in the service and have more control over the services they receive.

However, service users often experience problems in making use of complaints procedures.

Research by Finnegan and Clarke in 2005 identified that:

- 76% of staff agreed or strongly agreed with the statement that "very few service users use the formal complaints procedure".
- 82% agreed with the statement that service users "do not understand the process."
- 76% agreed with the statement "they do not understand their rights."

How?

Comments from staff involved in this research about the lack of use of complaints procedures included the following:

"Service users just don't like complaining. I can see why they wouldn't because I don't think I would feel at ease doing that if I was them. I'd be worried about being seen as a troublemaker I suppose, and you might be worried about how you might get treated afterwards."

"My worry is that they complain less and less because nothing is ever done…"

"The service users really do not feel that they can complain against someone who has power over their lives. It stays within the house and is not properly recorded or followed up."

"I know that every time there is an incident or complaint, everything should be written down but that is never the case."

(Finnegan and Clarke 2005)

Happless Care, Complaints Procedure

As part of our commitment to improving all our Care Services, any person wishing to make a complaint may do so, following the procedure outlined below:

1. Please make your complaint using form C7.0000.bd.XIX

2. If your complaint is made on behalf of a relative, then please use form C7,0090.SS.XXXX (part A) only. Part C and D should only be completed if your relative incurred any financial loss in relation to the complaint, but no personal injury.

3. If personal injury was incurred, please complete parts D, supplemented by form C3.0010…S. (ignoring part B).

4. Forms are available from floor 40, Bleak Tower, Middle of Nowhere. Please collect by hand.

5. Please collect the appropriate form prior to the incident in question.

How?

6. Please return the form promptly, making sure all fifty questions are answered in full, with supporting evidence from your GP and other referee.

7. Please complete your full name and address, and include a photograph of yourself and/or your loved one. This is to ensure that members of staff can be absolutely clear about who is making a nuisance of themselves.

8. Please obtain a receipt of postage, though a Microchip trace may be the only means of ensuring the complaint will not get completely and entirely lost.

9. If you do not have any response within 12 months of making your complaint, please complete form ZZ.23,000,SSI

Forms are available in a variety of languages, though it is doubtful if these can be found anywhere at all.

Complaints procedures can further disempower people.

"HAPPY TO HELP"

(Basnett and Maclean 2000)

Making Connections: Collective Action

Collectivism is seen a key to empowerment (see for example Yorkshire and Humber Empowerment Partnership 2011). It is certainly the key to macro approaches to empowerment. It can, however, be one of the most significant challenges to contemporary social workers required to engage and work with service users on an individual level. Ewart and Hindley (2011: 28) warn that we need to *"recognise the dangers of individualism which can divide groups and communities and render them powerless."*

The value of collectivism and supporting people to make connections is highlighted by the service users quoted in Branfield and Beresford (2006):

The more we network, the more powerful we can become.

Making links and connections makes us stronger.

How?

We need a collective national voice. If we are to succeed, we need stronger collective grass roots activism.

It is important to recognise that, whilst making connections with others who have similar experiences can be empowering for some people in itself, Ewart and Hindley (2011: 20) state that collectivism needs to achieve something:

"it's not just about bringing people together, they need to see some change and development coming out of their actions."

To maximise the fact that making connections can raise consciousness, help skill development and promote empowerment, practitioners should:

- work with service users to identify who is there to provide emotional and moral support to the service user
- consider ways of helping people to extend their circles of support
- encourage and enable service users to meet with others in similar situations
- make links with local groups and provide information about these to service users
- support the development of user led groups

Personalisation and Empowerment

Personalisation is a key component of contemporary social work practice. Stressed in current Government policy, it is being implemented across a changing landscape and is often referred to in transformational terms.

Arguments for personalisation include references to it being a key method of empowerment in contemporary social care. For example, Alzheimer Scotland (2011) assert that personalisation empowers individuals and families to direct their own services and their own lives.

Towell (2008) proposes a framework of three building blocks which demonstrate the way in which personalisation is a key aspect of promoting citizenship and empowerment.

How?

Civil Society

Government

SELF DETERMINATION

INCLUSION

Citizenship and Empowerment

PERSONALISED SUPPORT

Service System

Towell (2008) goes on to show the way in which these building blocks provide a framework around which to array the 12 key elements in national strategies for change:

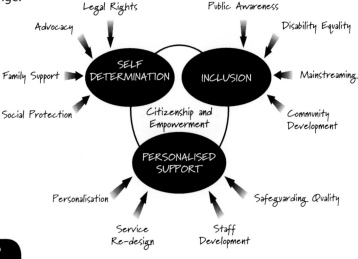

How?

Direct Payments and Personal Budgets

One practical application of the personalisation agenda is the development of personal budgets and direct payments. Direct payments are available to people who have been assessed as eligible for free social care by their local authority. The payments are given to the individual (or someone acting on their behalf) so that they can arrange and buy their own care rather than use traditional services provided by the local authority.

Personal budgets are based on personal need, they can be paid directly to the service user or managed by someone else on their behalf. Personal budgets may be taken as direct payments.

Direct payments, arguably represent one of the most practical tools for empowerment currently available in social work practice.

Empowerment and anti-oppressive practice

According to Hepworth et al (2010: 414) empowerment *"assumes that issues of power (and powerlessness) are inextricably linked to the experiences of oppression".*

The word oppression has its roots in Latin. It comes from the word opprimere which means to press on or press against. As such it suggests being pressed on and flattened – not being allowed to grow and develop. Looking at oppression in this way gives a very visual image of what it is like to be oppressed.

How?

Anti-oppressive practice seeks to both identify and challenge the mechanisms of oppression in order to empower individuals and groups. Contemporary writers recognise the links between this 'recognising and challenging' approach and empowerment. For example, Singh and Cowden (2009) argue that social workers should be seen as *"transformative intellectuals who do not succumb to power, but engage in uncovering, confronting and resisting power."*

Identifying oppression: Enabling people to recognise the way that they are oppressed is a key aspect of empowerment practice. Gardner (2011) suggests that practitioners must encourage service users to understand the connections between their own circumstances and the broader socio-political context in which they exist.

Challenging oppression: Seeking to challenge oppression is also a key aspect of empowerment – Zastrow (2010: 52) states that *"empowerment focussed social workers seek a more equitable distribution of resources and power among the various groups in society."*

Working in an anti-oppresive way, recognising and challenging oppression is an essential aspect of empowerment

Encouraging Hopefulness

The importance of people retaining a sense of hope has long been recognised as vital in mental health social work. The recovery model, for example, refers to the importance of the service user having someone who will hold a "candle of hope". People who achieve 'recovery' relate the importance of having people around them who continue to hope and convey a sense of confidence that recovery will eventually occur.

The cognitive model of depression (Beck et al 1979) demonstrates the importance of hope in breaking the "vicious cycle" of depression. Beck's model is often likened to the process of learned helplessness which demonstrates the fact that hope and positivity can assist in empowerment.

How?

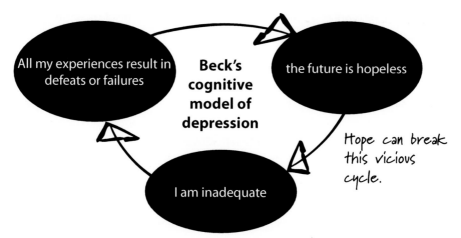

All my experiences result in defeats or failures

Beck's cognitive model of depression

the future is hopeless

I am inadequate

Hope can break this vicious cycle.

The concept of 'Hopeful Social Work Practice' has been developed in Australia where hope has been identified as a central feature in working with people with physical illness, acquired physical disabilities, medical conditions and mental health problems (Darlington and Bland 1999).

111

Hopeful social work is seen as a multi-dimensional construct recognising the following crucial elements of hope (Miller and Powers 1988: 8):

→ mutality affiliation: having a sense of belonging
→ sense of the possible: seeing things as possible
→ avoidance of absolutising: not imposing rigid conditions on 'hoped for' situations
→ anticipation: looking forward to a positive future
→ achieving goals
→ psychological well being and coping
→ sense of freedom
→ reality-surveillance optimism: searching for clues that confirm maintaining hope is feasible
→ mental and physical activation: maintaining activity to maintain hope

How?

Although 'hopeful social work practice' is not a phrase widely used in social work in the UK, the growth of interest in spirituality and social work is closely related.

It would be useful for social workers in the UK to consider the development of hopeful practice, especially in the current climate. Not least because as Stanford (2011) asserts, hopeful social work practice can assist social workers struggling in the current climate to maintain their professional focus and values in their day to day practice.

Developing Positive Attitude and Practices

It is widely accepted that attitude impacts on emotions. Positive attitudes have a positive impact on emotional wellbeing and a positive effect on feelings of personal empowerment, developing the 'power within'.

A whole industry has built itself up around the power of positive thinking. However, social workers often under estimate the importance of positive thinking in empowerment.

Henry Ford is attributed with saying: *"If you think you can or you think you can't........ You're right!"*

Negative	**Realistic**	**Positive**
It will **never** happen	It **could** happen	It **will** happen

How?

Top Tips for Positive Thinking

Social workers work in very difficult situations. This can mean they find positive thinking more difficult. In the current climate of scarce resources social workers very often find themselves having to focus on the negatives at work. Simply to obtain basic services or to justify any form of intervention the worst possible picture has to be painted. So whilst some of the following tips might sound very trite - do think about them carefully. You can assist service users to develop positive thinking, and it wouldn't do any harm for practitioners to develop their own positive thinking.

- Smile regularly.
  Develop your sense of humour.

- List the positives in your life -
  think about everything good.

- Try positive visualisation.

Social work in the current climate can create a negative thinking pattern. We need to actively consider how to support service users in developing and maintaining positive thinking.

- List the negatives - don't dwell on what they are but rather think about which ones you can change immediately, which ones you can change in the longer term, and accept those things which you cannot change.

- Let go of any negative feelings you have towards someone else - the negative thoughts hurt you more than anyone else.

- Surround yourself with positivity - listen to positive music, watch positive films, look at positive images. The impact of the senses on your mood and thought processes cannot be underestimated.

- Maintain a solution focussed approach.

- Consider social work approaches which have a positive view - such as strengths perspectives.

- Look for the opportunities in every difficulty.

How?

Positive Approaches: Appreciating the small things

The issues which social workers work with are often entrenched over a number of years and generally involve a range of complex factors. It can be easy to lose sight of achievements and positive change within this. Sometimes peoples needs and difficulties are so significant that small achievements are not recognised. Social workers can develop a cynical approach, which may be communicated, albeit unconsciously, to service users.

It is important for social workers to maintain a positive attitude to practice. Part of this will involve recognising that complex and difficult situations will not change overnight. Practitioners need to notice and appreciate every step that is taken - every positive in the work they do, and they need to encourage service users to recognise even small positive changes.

every journey begins with a single step.

(McKinnon 1998)

117

Helping Service Users to Develop Resources

Empowerment involves supporting people to develop a range of personal resources including:

Confidence:
Service users need to have confidence which relates closely to 'power within'. Confidence building can be a difficult and slow task. Ways to enhance confidence can include:

- joining with others who have had similar experiences and who have successfully changed their life positively

- individuals choosing an aspect of their life they want to change so there is a good chance of this being achieved

- encouraging a person to have a supporter or advocate present when they raise an issue of concern to them.

How?

A 'voice':

When a service user expresses something about their own life, practitioners and services should listen. Sometimes it can be difficult to 'listen' to the service user's voice because there is so much 'background noise' (or so many other voices). People can be so poor at listening effectively to a service user that having a voice may need to involve the person having an advocate.

Problem solving approach:

The service user will need to recognise that practical difficulties could arise in seeking to change their own life in the way they would like to. To achieve their goal, they will need to adopt a problem solving or solution focussed attitude.

Personal resources:

As discussed, supporting service users to develop their personal resolve and maintain a hopeful outlook is an important aspect of empowerment.

Empowerment and the Dignity of Risk

One of the key aspect of empowering people is that people need to be allowed to take risks and make their own choices. It sounds obvious, but:

- services have often in the past been too protective of people

- services have always sought to minimise or eliminate any risk of harm (emotional or physical harm)

- the attempt to eliminate all risk undermines people's dignity and inhibits opportunities for personal development and growth

- care environments that reduce risk as much as possible result in impoverished environments

- good risk assessments balance people's nights with consideration of risk and consequences

> *the notion that one has options from which to choose is often more important than the particular option one initially selects.* (Anthony 2000)

How?

The governing principle behind good approaches to risk is that people have the right to live their lives to the full as long as that does not stop others from doing the same.
(Department of Health 2008)

The aim should be for services to support people to take measured risks and to choose for themselves where possible how to live their own lives. As people are supported to develop and extend their skills, the risks associated should be evaluated to see if the person can extend their level of independence.

Risk taking is an integral part of daily life and is a significant route to supporting service users to maintain a sense of achievement and fulfilment. If it is handled in a planned and conscious way, it can be a great springboard for all.

We all take risks every time we step out of the front door, get in or drive a car, light a cigarette if we smoke, drink alcohol and so on, so why do services sometimes prevent their users from having the same choices?

The idea that there is dignity in risk is also sometimes referred to as the 'right to failure'. By taking away all risks from people, they can be denied the right to self determination - to decide for themselves how they want to live their life, even if the choices they make may not always be the 'best' ones.

Empowering people to take risks is not just about 'allowing' or 'permitting' actions to occur. It involves:

- Examination of one's own values to the action the person wants to take (what is your view on smoking? What about people involved in certain sexual activities? etc)
- Discussion about the whole range of choices which are available to the person, as well as the possible consequences (both positive and negative) of making certain choices
- Explaining to others why you are doing this as other people may be challenged by empowerment when it actually happens in this way
- Continuing to support the person, even if they make the choice you may not have expected, and even (or maybe especially) if they experience those negative consequences.

How?

Health and Safety and the 'Duty of Care'

Professionals and services working from a risk overse approach often quote health and safety or the duty of care when making risk overse plans. However, it is important to note that *"the Health and Safety Executive endorses a service approach to risk, so that health and safety legislation does not prevent reasonable activity."* (Department of Health 2010). In addition, the duty of care needs to be balanced with the 'duty to involve', which was implemented across England in 2009.

The Department of Health (2010) recommend that practitioners should:
- develop positive thinking about risk
- never assume risks because of factors such as diagnosis or service use
- ensure that risk assessment is proportionate to individual circumstances
- take a whole systems approach to risk
- recognise that over protection leads to people being placed at risk of being denied a fulfilling life

Critically reflective practice

Jan Fook is perhaps the most well known contemporary writer on reflective practice in social work. Fook's writing on reflective practice (eg: 2002) emphasises the vital importance of the practitioner reflecting on power dynamics and the implications of these. Fook's model is essentially based on a 3 step process.

 Telling the narrative

 Deconstructing the situation

 Reconstructing the situation

 How?

Telling the Narrative

Effectively this is where the practitioner is describing the practice and what was occurring in the situation chosen as the critical incident.

Deconstruction

This is essentially a stage of reflective questioning exploring the practice. Fook focuses on exploring issues of power and how power is constructed.

Reconstruction

This is the stage of planning future practice and putting the plans into action. Fook refers to redeveloping practice. Again she refers to paying particular attention to power relationships and how power structures and relationships can be changed to be more emancipatory.

Reflecting on your use of power and on your ability to apply empowerment in practice is vital. Fook's model can be helpful in reminding practitioners to reflect on power. In many ways reflective practice is about a process of dynamic questioning, considering the following questions might assist you in developing your reflection on empowerment:

Definitions

- How do I define power?
- How do I define empowerment?
- Which other definitions of power and empowerment do I find useful? Why?

Ongoing development of your practice

- What opportunities can I take to keep on learning about power and empowerment?

How?

- In what ways can I keep these issues on my agenda and that of my colleagues?
- Do I use supervision effectively to reflect on power?
- Who and what can help me to keep developing?

Considering service users situations

- In what ways was the service user powerful?
- In what ways were they disempowered?
- How did they feel about me coming into their life?
- How would I feel if our roles were reversed?
- How did I communicate their expertise on their own needs, what their rights are and what options they have?
- Did we both understand these things in the same way?
- How did I empower the person?
- Did I disempower them in any way? How? Why?

General practice

- What aspects of my practice are empowering?
- What aspects of my practice are disempowering?
- How do I use the various components of empowerment?
- What aspects of empowerment do I find most challenging? Why?
- How do I express my personal commitment to empowerment?

Adopting a critically reflective approach to social work practice in general can assist in empowerment, particularly as it highlights power differentials and enables practitioners to reconstruct power. It is also important to adopt a reflective approach to empowerment - which involves practitioners exploring a range of questions.

How?

Empowerment: Cake or spiders web?

We have referred to the value of considering empowerment in terms of its key ingredients. It is important to recognise though there are dangers to this approach and breaking theories down into component parts can lead to mechanistic practice.

One of the dangers in breaking empowerment down is that where a practitioner does one of the things we have discussed they may claim to have 'empowered' a service user. In maintaining the recipe analogy - empowerment is a complex multi-layered cake. The cake cannot be made without all (or at least most) the ingredients.

Whilst it can be useful to consider the 'ingredients' when looking at what specific practical actions social workers can take, it is vital to remember that empowerment is not the icing on the cake. It's the cake!

Throughout this section of the Pocket Guide it is clear that there are links between the different components we have highlighted. In many ways, a visual representation of empowerment could look like a spider's web with links between the many different elements.

Regular reference is made to 'networks of power' and the construction of power. Thinking then about a spider's web and how it is constructed around a range of 'networks' provides a useful visual image of empowerment. In constructing webs, spiders often find the most difficult thread is the first and until a number of threads are in place, the web is vulnerable to being blown away. Just like empowerment!

How?

Empowerment: the never ending journey?

The Yorkshire and Humber Empowerment Partnership (2011) describe empowerment as a journey. They make the point that we are all at different stages on the journey towards empowerment.

Generally when we are going on a journey we plan to reach a particular destination. However, we think it is important to view empowerment as a never ending journey. Those practitioners that claimed to have empowered people generally have a very simplistic view of empowerment.

So we end this Pocket Guide almost where we started this section - maybe as a never ending journey, empowerment *is* an aspirational rather than achievable goal in contemporary social work. However, there are approaches we can use and routes we can take which will make the journey a more useful and empowering one.

See the empowerment journey as one to be enjoyed and shared with the service user. There may be times when you take the driving seat for various reasons, but on the whole the idea of empowerment is that the service user should be in the driving seat, or at the very least, directing the journey.

How?

References

Alzheimer Scotland (2011) *Let's get personal: Personalisation and Dementia.* Available online at www.alzscot.org/pages/policy/report-personalisation-and-dementia.htm. Accessed 29.4.11.

Anthony, W. (2000) A *Recovery oriented service system: Setting some system level standards.* Psychiatric Rehabilitation Journal, 24(2) pp 159-168.

Association of Directors of Social Services (2005) *Safeguarding Adults: A National Framework of Standards for good practice and outcomes in adult protection work.* (London) ADSS.

Bar-On, A. (2002) *Restoring Power to Social Work Practice.* British Journal of Social Work 32(8) pp 997-1014.

Barker, R.L. (2009) *The Social Work Dictionary.* (5th Edition) (Washington) NASW Press.

Basnett, F. and Maclean, S. (2000) *The Value Base in Practice: An NVQ Related Reference Guide for Staff Working with Older People*. (Rugeley) Kirwin Maclean Associates.

Beck, A.T., Rush, A.J., Shaw, B.F. and Emery, G. (1979) *Cognitive Therapy of Depression*. (New York) Guildford.

Beirne, M. (2006) *Empowerment and Innovation: Managers, Principles and Reflective Practice*. (Cheltenham) Edward Eglar Publishing.

Bernhagen, P. (2002) *Power: Making sense of an elusive concept*. Available online at http://docs.google.com/viewer?a=v&q=cache:p2hcHC6UOgEJ. Accessed 26.8.11.

Betts Adams., Matto, C., LeCroy, C.W. (2009) *Limitations of evidence-based practice for social work education: unpacking the complexity*. Available online at http://findarticles.com/p/articles/mi_hb3060/is_2_45/ai_n35624095/pg_9. Accessed 29.9.11.

Branfield, F. and Beresford, P. (2006) *Making User involvement work: supporting service user networking and knowledge.* Joseph Rowntree Foundation. Available online at www.jrf.org.uk/publications/making_user_involvement_work_supporting_service_user_networking_and_knowledge. Accessed 13.10.11.

Cameron, C. (2007) *Social Pedagogy and the Children's Workforce.* Available online at www.communitycare.co.uk/Articles/2007/08/08/105392/social_pedagogy_and_the_childrens_workforce.htm. Accessed 19.1.10.

Chanan, G. and Miller, C. (2010) *The Big Society: How it could work.* (London) PACES.

Clarke, J. Gewirtz, S. and McLaughlin, E. (Eds) (2000) *New Managerialism, New Welfare.* (London) Sage.

Commission for Social Care Inspection (2008) *Safeguarding adults: A study of the effectiveness of arrangements to safeguard adults from abuse.* (London) CSCI.

Cooper, B. (2011) *Criticality and Reflexivity: Best Practice in Uncertain Environments.* In Sedel, J., Matthews, S. McCormick, M. and Morgan, A. (Eds) Professional Development in Social Work: Complex Issues in Practice. (Oxon) Routledge.

Croft, S. and Beresford, P. (1992) *The Politics of Participation.* Critical Social Policy, 35. pp 20-44.

Darlington, Y. and Bland, R. (1999) *Strategies for Encouraging and Maintaining hope among people living with serious mental illness.* Australian Social Work, 52. pp 17-24.

Department of Health (2008) *Transforming Adult Social Care.* (London) The Stationery Office.

Department of Health (2009) *Written Ministerial Statement. Government response to the consultation on safeguarding adults: the review of the no secrets guidance.* Available online at http://webarchive.nationalarchives.gov.uk/+/

www.dh.gov.uk/en/Consultations/Responsestoconsultations/DH_111286. Accessed 1.10.11.

Department of Health (2010) *Practical Approaches to Safeguarding and Personalisation*. (London) Department of Health.

Deutsch, M., Coleman, P.T., and Marcus, E. (2006) (eds) *The Handbook of Conflict Resolution*. (San Francisco) Jossey Bass.

Dominelli, L. (2002) *Anti-Oppressive Social Work Theory and Practice*. (Basingstoke) Palgrave Macmillan.

Duluth Model (2011) *Home of the Duluth Model*. Available online at www.theduluthmodel.org. Accessed 4.10.11.

Ewart, B. and Hindley, A. (2011) *Is the time right for a rebirth of true community development?* In Yorkshire and Humber Empowerment Partnership (2011) Empowerment: Reflections from Yorkshire and Humber. Available online at www.yhep.org.uk. Accessed 29.9.11.

Finnegan, P. and Clarke, S. (2005) *One Law for All? The Impact of the Human Rights Act on People with Learning Difficulties. (*London) Values into Action.

Fook J. (2002) *Social Work: Critical Theory and Practice.* (London) Sage.

Foucoult, M. (1977) *Discipline and Punishment.* (London) Tavistock.

Friere, P. (1970) *Pedagogy of the Oppressed.* (New York) Herder and Herder.

French, J. and Raven, B.H. (1959) *The bases of social power.* In Cartwright (ed) Studies in Social Power. pp 150-167. (Ann Arbor) Institute for Social Research.

Gallagher, M. (2010) *Engaging with Involuntory service users in social work.* Available online at http://docs.google.com/viewera&q=cache:mmzd4wGYHkoj.www.socialwork.ed.ac.uk/_data/assets/pdf-file/0011/37874. Accessed 13.10.11.

Gardner, A. (2011) *Personalisation in Social Work.* (Exeter) Learning Matters.

Gaventa, J. (2005) *Reflections of the uses of the 'Power Cube' Approach for Analyzing the Spaces, Places and Dynamics of Civil Society Participation and Engagement.* CFP Evaluation Series No.4.

General Social Care Council (2009) *The Teaching and Assessment of Safeguarding within Approved PQ courses: Messages from the Annual monitoring reports of PQ programmes* (08/09). (London) GSCC.

Hepworth, D.H., Rooney, R.H., Dewberry Rooney, G., Strom-Gottfried, K. and Larsen, J. (2010) *Direct Social Work Practice: Theory and Skills.* (Belmont) Cengage Learning.

Higham, P. (2005) *What is important about social work and social care?* Available online at www.ssrg.org.uk/assembly/files/patriciahigham.pdf. Accessed 26.10.09.

Hinson, S. and Healey, R. (2003) *Building Political Power. Prepared for the State Strategies Fund Convening.* Grassroots Policy Project.

Inner London Probation Service (1993) *Working with Difference: A Positive and Practical Guide to Anti-Discriminatory Practice Teaching.* (London) Inner London Probation Service.

International Federation of Social Workers and International Association of Schools of Social Work (2000) *International Definition of Social Work.* Available online at www.ifsw.org/f38000138.html. Accessed 1.10.11.

International Federation of Social Workers (2011) *The Social Impact of the Financial Crisis: Project Papers.* Presented at IFSW Symposium. ENSACT Conference Brussels 10-13 April 2011.

Just Associates (2006) *Making Change Happen: Power. Concepts for Revisioning Power for Justice, Equality and Peace.* (Washington) Just Associates.

Kam, P.K. (2002) *From Disempowering to Empowering: Changing the practice of social service professionals with Older People.* Hallym International Journal of Aging. 4(2) pp 161-183.

Kendrick, A. (1998 online) *Who Do We Trust? The abuse of children living away from home in the United Kingdom.* Online at http://homepages.strath.ac.uk/~zns01101/ispcan.htm. Accessed 1.10.11.

Kreisberg, S. (1992) *Transforming Power: Domination, Empowerment and Education.* (Albany) State University of New York Press.

Livestrong.com (2011 online) *Accepting Powerlessness.* Available online at www.livestrong.com/article/14716_accepting_powerlessness. Accessed 18.6.11.

Lopez, J. (2011) *Contemporary Sociological Theories.* Available online at http://docs.google.com/viewer?a=v&q=cache:JdxbXU3vSGsJ:ssms.socialsciences.uottawa.ca/vfs/horde/offre_cours/0028710205. Accessed 1.8.11.

Lukes, S. (ed) (1986) *Power.* (Oxford) Basil Blackwell.

Lukes, S. (2004) *Power: A Radical View.* (2nd edition) Palgrave Macmillan.

Lum, D. (2010) *Culturally Competent Practice: A framework for understanding diverse groups and justice issues.* (Belmont) Brooks / Cole.

Maclean, S. and Harrison, R. (2010) *Social Care: The Common Knowledge Base. A Pic 'n' Mix Guide.* (Rugeley) Kirwin Maclean Associates Ltd.

Matthews, S. McCormick, M. and Morgan, A. (2001) (Eds) *Professional Development in Social Work: Complex Issues in Practice.* (Abingdon) Routledge.

McKinnon, K.D. (1998) *Coping with Caring: the dangers of Chronic Stress and Burnout.* Available online at www.charityvillage.com/cv/research/rpersdvl.html. Accessed 30.12.10.

Miller, J.F. and Powers, M.J. (1988) *Development of an Instrument to Measure Hope.* Nursing Research Vol 37(1) pp 6-10.

Mooney, A., Stillwell Peccei, J., Labelle, S., Henrikson, B., Eppler, E., Irwin, A., Pichler, P., Preece, S. and Soden, S. (2011) *Language, Society and Power: An Introduction*. (3rd edition) (Oxon) Routledge.

Morgenthau, H.J. (1978) P*olitics among Nations: The struggle for power and peace*. 5th edition. (New York) Knopf.

Napier, A. (undated) *Empowerment Theory*. Available online at http://docs.google.com/viewer?a=v&q=cache:zRiyHU4Ju@j:www:malone.edu/media/1/7/71/Empowerment_Presentation_A_Napier.S06.pdf. Accessed 1.10.11.

NSPCC (2011 online) *Defining Child Abuse*. Online at http://www.nspcc.org.uk/Inform/cpsu/helpandadvice/organisations/defining/definingchildabuse_wda60692.html. Accessed 1.10.11.

Nye, J.S. (2004) *Soft Power: The Means to Success in World Politics*. (New York) Public Affairs.

Penhale, B. and Parker, J. (2008) *Working with Vulnerable Adults*. (Abingdon) Routledge.

Powercube.net (2011 online) *Power cube: Understanding power for social change*. Online at www.powercube.net. Accessed 10.9.11.

Rankin, P. (2006) *Exploring and Describing the Strength / Empowerment Perspective in Social Work*. Available online at www.bemidjistate.edu/academics/publications/social_work_journal/issue14/articles/rankin.htm. Accessed 7.10.11.

Robbins, S.P., Chartterjee, P. and Canda, E.R. (1998) *Contemporary Human Behaviour Theory*. (Boston) Allyn and Bacon.

Rodgers, J. (2003) *Reason, Conflict and Power: Modern Political and Social Thought from 1688 to the present*. (Oxford) University Press of America.

Saleeby, D. (1996) *The Strengths perspective in social work practice: extensions and cautions.* Social Work 41. pp 296-305.

SCIE (2003) *Learning and Teaching in Social Work Education: Assessment.* (London) SCIE.

Scottish Government (2005) T*he Role of the Social Worker in the 21st Century: A Literature Review.* (Edinburgh) Scottish Government.

Seabury, B., Seabury, B. and Garvin, C.D. (2011) *Foundations of Interpersonal Practice in Social Work: Promoting Completence in Generalist Practice.* (London) Sage.

Shivers, J.S. (2001) *Leadership and Groups in Recreational Service.* (Cranbury) Rosemont Publishing.

Singh, G. and Cowden, S. (2009) *The Social Worker as intellectual.* European Journal of Social Work. 2009 pp1-5.

Smith, R. (2010) *Social Work, Risk, Power. (Sociological Research online).*

Available online at http://www.socresonline.org.uk/15/1/4.html. Accessed 28.4.11.

Snell, J. (2007) *The Friday Debate: Should social workers dress up or dress down for work?* Available online at www.communitycare.co.uk./articles/31/08/2007. Accessed 29.9.11.

Social Care Institute for Excellence (2009) *At A Glance 01: Learning Together to Safeguard Children: a 'systems' model for case reviews.* (London) SCIE.

Social Platform (2010) *Briefing Number 33: Annual Theme 2010 on Care.* (Brussels) Social Platform.

Spykman, N.J. (1942) *American Strategy in World Politics.* (New York) Harcourt Brace.

Stanford, S.N. (2011) *Constructing Moral Responses to Risk: A Framework for Hopeful Social Work Practice.* British Journal of Social Work online March 24, 2011.

ThemPra Social Pedagogy Community Interest Society (2009) *Social Pedagogy: Theory meets practice.* Available online at www.socialpedagogy.co.uk/concepts.htm. Accessed 19.1.10.

Thompson, N. (2001) *Anti-discriminatory practice.* In Davies, M. (Ed) The Blackwell Companion to Social Work (2nd Edition) (Oxford) Blackwell Publishing.

Tolan, J. (2003) *Skills in person-centred counselling and psychotherapy.* (London) Sage.

Towell, D. (2008) *People with Intellectual Disabilities: Exploring Strategies for Achieving Equal Citizenship.* Presentation to the International Association for the Scientific Study of Intellectual Disability, Cape Town. August 2008.

Tuitt, W. (2010) *Power and Policy: Lessons for Leaders in Government and Business.* (California) Praeger.

Veneklasen, L. and Miller, V. (2002 reprinted 2007) *A New Weave of Power, People and Politics: the action guide for advocacy and citizen participation.* (Oklahoma) World Neighbours.

Walker, S. and Beckett, C. (2003) *Social Work Assessment and Intervention.* (2nd edition). (Lyme Regis) Russell House Publishing.

Warrin, B. (2010) *Safeguarding adults in Cornwall.* The Journal of Adult Protection, 12 (2) pp 39-42.

White, C. Holland, D. Marsland, D. and Oakes, O. (2003) *The identification of environments and cultures that promote the abuse of people with intellectual disabilities. A review of the literature.* Journal of Applied Research in Intellectual Disabilities, 16. pp 1-9.

Williamson, M. (1992) *Our Greatest Fear.* Available online at http://explorersfoundation.org/glyphery/122_html. Accessed 22.3.11.

Yorkshire and Humber Empowerment Partnership (2011) *Empowerment: Reflections from Yorkshire and Humber*. Available online at www.yhep.org.uk. Accessed 29.9.11.

Zastrow, C. (2010) *Introduction to Social Work and Social Welfare: Empowering People*. (10th edition) (Belmont) Cengage Learning.